Dedication

This book is dedicated to the beloved Imām of our time (ʿaj). May Allah (swt) hasten his reappearance and help us to become his true companions.

Acknowledgments

Prophet Muḥammad (ṣ): The pen of a writer is mightier than the blood of a martyr.

True reward lies with Allah, but we would like to sincerely thank the efforts of Shaykh Salim Yusufali, Brother Aliakbar Shaheidari, Sisters Sabika Mithani, Fatemah Mithani, Amna Hussain, Asieh Zarghami, Zahra Sabur, Sajeda Merchant, Kisae Nazar, Fathema Abidi, Fatemeh Eslami, Fatima Hussain, Fatemah Meghji, Zehra Abbas and Abeda Khimji. We would especially like to thank Jamal an-Nashr Publications for their artwork and contributions. May Allah bless them in this world and the next.

Marḥūmīn Dedication

Please recite a Sūrah al-Fātiḥah for Marḥūmah Salma Kassam,
a wonderful mother and dedicated teacher of Islam.

Preface

Prophet Muḥammad (ṣ): Nurture and raise your children in the best way. Raise them with the love of the Prophets and the Ahl al-Bayt (ʿa).

Literature is an influential form of media that often shapes the thoughts and views of an entire generation. Therefore, in order to establish an Islamic foundation for future generations, there is a dire need for compelling Islamic literature. Over the past several years, this need has become increasingly prevalent throughout Islamic centers and schools everywhere. Due to the growing dissonance between parents, children, society, and the teachings of Islam and the Ahl al-Bayt (ʿa), this need has become even more pressing. Al-Kisa Foundation, along with its subsidiary, Kisa Kids Publications, was conceived in an effort to help bridge this gap with the guidance of ʿulamāʾ and the help of educators. We would like to make this a communal effort and platform. Therefore, we sincerely welcome constructive feedback and help in any capacity.

The goal of *My Allah Series* is to help children form a loving and positive relationship with their Creator and leave them wanting to know more about Allah. We hope that you and your children enjoy these books and use them as a means to achieve this goal, inshāʾAllāh.

We pray to Allah to give us the strength and tawfīq to perform our duties and responsibilities.

With Duʿās,
Nabi R. Mir (Abidi)

My Allah Series

Allah is the Most Wise

Kisa Kids Publications

AL-KISA FOUNDATION
WWW.KISAKIDS.ORG

Parents' Corner

وَاللَّهُ عَلِيمٌ حَكِيمٌ

And Allah is All-Knowing, All-Wise
(Sūrah an-Nisāʾ, Verse 26)

Dear Parents/Guardians,

It is possible that older children who difiantly question Islam may have ideological problems that stem from their lack of understanding and belief in Allah's wisdom. Their belief in Allah's wisdom may be weak, and therefore, they do not trust Him to do what is best for them. As a result, they have difficulty following Allah's orders.

It is vital and of utmost importance that parents strengthen children's understanding of Allah's wisdom at a young age. It is important to continuously remind them that Allah created us and takes care of us; He wants us to become good Muslims, get closer to Him, and go to Jannah. Through these reminders, children will innately strengthen their love and trust in Allah deep in their hearts. Additionally, it is very important for parents to keep reminding themselves and their children that Allah is the Most Knowledgeable and always knows what is best for us, even though we might not always understand why.

If this understanding is strengthened in our children at a young age, inshāʾAllāh they will grow up to ask questions about their dīn in a positive manner, so that they can understand it better. They will become more confident and content with fulfilling their duties, such as ṣalāh, ḥijāb, and fasting, inshāʾAllāh.

We hope that *Allah is the Most Wise* will encourage your children to ponder upon Allah's wisdom and miracles and realize that He truly is the All-Wise.

With Duʿās,
Kisa Kids Publications

When you look at a tall building, you know the builder must be very smart. He must be an expert and know all about its different parts.

Have you ever seen how tall buildings are made?

When you see a beautiful piece of art, you know the artist must be very smart!

Who gave painters the hands they paint with?

When you see an airplane flying high above the trees,
you know the clever engineer knows a lot about machines.

Where would you go in an airplane?

When you see a farmer busy with his planting, you realize he must know a lot about farming.

What are some fruits a farmer grows?

But who made the birds, the trees, and the sun?
Of course Allah, the Mighty, the One.
Everywhere I turn and look with my two eyes,
I try to see how Allah is the Most Wise.

What are some other things Allah has created so perfectly?

When I look in the mirror, I see how Allah made me carefully.
If my eyes were under my feet, how would I be able to see?
Allah placed my hands, legs, and eyes exactly where they should be.
Thinking of every detail, He's the Most Wise, al-Ḥakīm!*

What would happen if your eyes were not on your head, but were on your hands and feet instead?

***Pronunciation Guide:**
Ḥ is a heavy "ha" sound that comes from the middle of the throat; ī is an elongated "e" sound, like "ee"

Allah gave me fingers to eat spaghetti and rice. Allah knows everything and is the Most Wise!

Try picking up something without your thumb, only using 4 fingers. What happens?

Allah gave me teeth to eat my meals and snacks.
The front teeth bite the food, and it gets chewed in the back.
This way, I can eat apples, chicken, and pies.
Allah knows everything, He is the Most Wise!

What are some things you eat using your teeth?

Allah gave me eyebrows so sweat doesn't drop into my eyes.
Allah knows everything; He is the most Wise!

What games make you sweat?

Look at the stork with its extra long beak.
It can catch fish from the water, even when it's deep!
The more I look, the more I see
how Allah made the world so perfectly!

What are some other amazing and perfect things Allah created?

Family Involvement!

From this story, your children learned how Allah is the Most Wise. To emphasize the main objective of this book, please try to do the following:

- Reread *Allah is the Most Wise* with your children. Young children crave repetition and become more familiar with a book the more they read it.
- When your children point out something that fascinates them or that is "cool," talk about how Allah gave wisdom to the person who made it.
- When watching a plane pass by or seeing tall towers, remind your children that Allah gave the creators of those items the ability to do so.
- When you go to the zoo or see a beautiful sunrise, remark on the wisdom of Allah in how every creation is created so perfectly.
- Remind your children to say SubḥānAllāh — all glory is due to Allah — when they see something beautiful (e.g., a pretty flower, the birds, beautiful scenery, etc.).
- Remind your children how Allah has created each of us in a special way.
- As your children get older, they will learn more science (e.g., how the earth rotates around the sun). All of these conversations are a way to bring up the wisdom of Allah and how each and every thing in the world was created perfectly through Allah's wisdom.

Transliteration

Arabic has been transliterated according to the following key:

ء	a, u, i (initial form)	ز	z	ك	k	َ	a
ء	ʾ	س	s	ل	l	ُ	u
ب	b	ش	sh	م	m	ِ	i
ت	t	ص	ṣ	ن	n	ـَا	ā
ث	th	ض	ḍ	ه	h	ـُو	ū
ج	j	ط	ṭ	و	w (as a consonant)	ـِي	ī
ح	ḥ	ظ	ẓ	ي	y (as a consonant)		
خ	kh	ع	ʿ	ة	ah (without iḍāfah)		
د	d	غ	gh	ة	at (with iḍāfah)		
ذ	dh	ف	f	ال	al-		
ر	r	ق	q				